OLD GODS

If Rainer Maria Rilke shared a notebook with Frank Stanford, something like Clifford Brooks's lyric would climb to the surface. Changing pace from soft whirls to sharp, jagged lines and then sinews, the poems travel through Southern life, music, love, memory, despair, hope. This whirling motion carved from places and worn spaces is as sensitive as it is raw. The back porch has enough space for Bacchus and Bach; the heart has enough space elegy and rapture; "the sky is a nightgown"—and this book is its stunning horizon.

—Alina Stefanescu, author of
Dor and *Ribald*

Clifford Brooks is a poet of awe, of what the Greeks termed *agape*—to be open-mouthed with wonder. These observant, powerfully imaged poems are also open-hearted and embracing of the physical and familial realms, the wild and the domestic, and the possibilities for metaphysical and spiritual transformation. Gentle and intense, there is a wisely modest quality that the last line of the very first poem invokes for me so well: "I do not know how words capture / trees." Yet capture he does in these valuable poems included in his newest book, *Old Gods*.

—Stuart Dischell, award-winning author
of *Good Hope Road*

Clifford Brooks is a poet who just can't help it: poems fly out of him like weightless jewels, like the hummingbirds he writes of so cannily. The poetry in *Old Gods* is ebullient, alive, and blessedly uncategorizable. It is casually populated by totems of the rural South that also happen to be real, and that Brooks knows intimately. *Old Gods* says essential things in new ways, while remaining tied to individual human vision, in a voice confident and shy, audacious, and tender. It is a joy to read.

—Jeffrey Skinner, author of *6.5 Practices
of Moderately Successful Poets*

Also by Clifford Brooks

POETRY

The Draw of Broken Eyes & Whirling Metaphysics

Exiles of Eden

Athena Departs: Gospel of a Man Apart

OLD GODS

Poems

Clifford Brooks

MERCER UNIVERSITY PRESS
Macon, Georgia

MUP/ P678

Published by Mercer University Press
1501 Mercer University Drive
Macon, Georgia 31207

27 26 25 24 23   5 4 3 2 1

Books published by Mercer University Press are printed on acid-free paper that meets the requirements of the American National Standard for Information Sciences—Permanence of Paper for Printed Library Materials.

Printed and bound in the United States.
This book is set in Adobe Garamond with Georgia (display).
Cover/jacket design by Burt&Burt.

Library of Congress Cataloging-in-Publication Data
Names: Brooks, Clifford, author.
Title: Old gods : poems / Clifford Brooks.
Description: Macon, Georgia : Mercer University Press, [2023] | Summary: "This book deals with the redemptive power of words, addiction—the processing and walking beyond It. Autism and the thriving that comes from study as well as living. Difficulties of relationships. Facing a Dante's "midpoint of life" and looking back—then forward to God"— Provided by publisher.
Identifiers: LCCN 2023024568 | ISBN 9780881469066 (paperback)
Subjects: LCGFT: Poetry.
Classification: LCC PS3602.R644253 O43 2023 | DDC 811/.6—dc23/eng/20230607
LC record available at https://lccn.loc.gov/2023024568

For

John Fleming, Momma, Daddy, Alain Johannes,

Russ Howard, Ahna Phillips, and Father George Yandell

Contents

Acknowledgments

I struggled through the spectrum to get this book on paper. Right now, I sit in church (before service) to gain guidance with this note. Before I get into those who helped *Old Gods* beat my indulgence for self-sabotage, I wish to thank you—the reader. This is my third book, and you've fed my drive. Inspiration and the eating need to write fuel my fire, but you keep my words between the ditches.

Thank you, Marc Jolley with Mercer University Press, for believing in this book. Thank you, Skye Jackson, for your early work editing *Old Gods*. Thank you to NPR for allowing me a show, and the Southern Collective Experience for providing a safe harbor to find peace. Without the wonderful people of the SCE, my family, and diehard friends there'd be no "me" to do "this."

Thank you, *Crab Orchard Review, The Tusculum Review, Otoliths, The Pedestal Magazine, The Shore Poetry, Porridge Magazine, and Louisiana Literature* for getting behind this collection. It is an honor to see my work mature with your help.

Finally, thank you, Alain Johannes, for your musical influence these last twenty years, and co-writing "Natasha's Indelible Pedestal."

I would like to write a poem about the world that has in it
nothing fancy.
But it seems impossible.

—Mary Oliver

Flourishing a white-feather fan
lazily, I go naked in green forests.

Soon, I've hung my hat on a cliff,
Set my hair loose among pine winds.

—Li Po

I think of a pyramid and an hourglass a voice

that gives off its own light
my life I love it
in the dark
under that water of my shadow music

—Frank Stanford

My life is not this steeply sloping hour,
in which you see me hurrying.
Much stands behind me; I stand before it like a tree;
I am only one of my many mouths,
and at that, the one that will be still the soonest.

I am the rest between two notes,
which are somehow always in discord
because Death's note wants to climb over—
but in the dark interval, reconciled,
they stay there trembling.
And the song goes on, beautiful.

—Rainer Maria Rilke

Pruning a Dream

for Robert Gwaltney

What is it about a tree?
In my hand, a pruning tool
necessary for the dream.

I am a gardener. Careless as a cricket,
anxiety anchored
on the back of a beetle.

...

Boulders urge a river
around us.
On water-slicked rocks,
cross-legged
and un-licked by life,
we don't cheapen
the silence
with speech.

Beside a berm,
stone is made by man
into a dam.
Water moccasin
breach its levy.
A snapping turtle hisses.
One blue heron
stands aloof.

Frogs croak so loudly
cicadas can't
be heard.

Birds create shadows
between light
and the ground. We wait,
then roll over
too late to see
sparrows.
Alone
with the sun.

...

Trees, frayed wicks
splay upward.
Burning green,
rain feeds,
and God waylays
decay.

Wind bends
a fir's fringes.
With enough,
there's a bending
of sentinels
over
blades of grass.

...

The forest—its precise nature
isn't set or studied.
It's easy to think what I do here
is important.

Leaves in a whirlpool behave like men
in a rut: Around and around
and around.

I do not know how trees capture
words.

Five Cities

Life, torture, a delightfully
dysfunctional orchard,
and my fruit road-ripe.
Drive:
An amicable accord
in a great house's
floorboards.
Roads lead darkly,
save the light
seeping between fingers.

Chattanooga: Big as a
brick shithouse, too tall
Jamaal and white lions—
we riot in this tumultuous spring.
The 'Noog shares its view
with the King of *I Have a Dream.*
A food desert,
so many skittish
in a gun-split city.

Jasper: South,
Sharp Top
juts up from marbled eggs.
A priest keeps faith there
like Steinbeck's
pearl of the world.
A cathedral of towering trees
back to life.
Behind a wooden bridge
an old troll dies.

*Athens: R*edemption rains
on shores, square blocks –
breasts the arches across Broad.
Feet beat the street
where my saints and madmen trod.
I trod still
until haints
howl me home.

Crawford: Sundown downtown
uncrowded Crawford.
The dealership, an old crown,
a castle closed.
Refitted, a barbecue joint.
My long, red car stops
in Lexington.

Lexington: Memory,
ceaseless.
Anonymity, attractive
but unnatural.
Myth and miles,
aces and bad hands,
traveling, moving,
cutting a straight line.

On the Floor with Terpsichore

Weightless girl,
sway and swirl—
   shoulders
back
and mind relaxed.
Don't hustle.
Warm muscles hug bone,
soul toned
for dancing.

Barely air between us,
not squeamish,
children of Jesus,
your form—seamless.
  Spin.
Society jealously
sits at our fringes.

Doubt decays
and our hips waylay
the idea
a good lady
never lays down.

Let's sashay   away.
Apsara,
lo que sera sera.
Waltz or tango?
Get up!   *Let go*!
  Leap up the wild doe.

Growl and scream,
"No one owns me!"
Because you are you
respected and adored,
envied and abhorred—
you who bravely dances.

This Weeping Affliction

Worry, memory
wound like an 8-day clock.
Awake—my will,
a fetching corpse
fidgeting—never still.

I do not ask you to understand.

Dawn, daybreak, the cock—
it makes my mouth lock
on the taste of adult candy.
Possessed, a quiet skeleton.
I do not listen.
Do not whisper my name.

I do not ask you to understand.

A skiff
of ragged veins and mercury,
my future hobbled.
Hungry, immediately
the morning
reminds me:
Addiction to actively
looking back
is anomie.

I do not ask you to understand.

Anomie

Blue lights, whoop-*whoop*,
cops, swerving, shouts.
An ant winkled out
by a baboon.
Lions before a fawn.
Blood drawn,
naked and scrawny.
Apathetic, parasitic,
a rubber spoon,
no bail money.

Anorexic, tremors, twitch,
scheming, barking.
Fourth arrest demands
undivided attention.
Inside: orange the equalizer,
shoes sans laces,
a decent lawyer,
one lovers, all Plexiglas faces.

This hinders
my career.
This endears me
to no one.

Twilight nears
windows
too low
to see stars.
Seventeen days,
prison without bars.
A clown fish
caught in anemone.

From the Lip of a Lake

God whips up
wind's memory,
holds it,
then whistles
through whippoorwills.

...

Wooden stairs, a maple-
bowed arbor,
placid water
cracks and waffles
perfect circles.

Baby spiders
feast on dragonflies.
A beast without a brood,
raising countless children.

Barren Mother Mary,
she witnesses
God in bending willows,
panacea for the diphtheria
of 12 terrible cycles.
Breathe.
The walkabout we need
pulls
like a toddler.

A Map of Old Mountains for Young Men

Scraaaaaaatch, a match ignites
across teeth chipped
from clenching.
Weathered men whisper:
The skin of disturbed youth
reflects the moon.
Babes stumble over
shadows cast by pines.

Shivering,
adulthood's fearful symmetry
limps into middle age.
Catatonic, laconic years
linger
like bad lovers.
Some burns go on.

Follow well-tread footsteps
away from coyotes,
shine stills, and poppy fields.
Wise wolves
weave long days,
not easy, low-hanging fruit.
Do not buy trouble:
An expensive,
unimpressive suit.

Time makes men desperate
for free space.
Where wild lives

civilized men
sprint,
apologizing
for nothing.

Bacchus Tries to Retire

Bacchus sits back with his dignity intact,
itching from the stitches of mismanagement.
"It is not romantic. It's avoidably tragic
to waste one's life as a drunk."
A demigod, semi-sod, speaks to his breed,
"Broken stereotypes are the addiction.
Fear, the artist's cruelest affliction."
Jaw squared, Bacchus still
bears the marks of cruel intention.

The barroom is poverty. Royalty repeating,
"I'm sorry. I'm sorry. I'm sorry."
His youth, middle age, my forties—centuries—
not all sad songs, not sad even mostly.
Still, havoc remains spiritually costly.
He whispers to no one: "You can't get it back.
Not a vagabond nor a god."
A moment of silence, the cross, and a nod.

"Ridin' stars, rusty pipes: Anything but free.
Inevitably kin note their family tree
drops another meth-addled apple.
Cidered inside a fermented chapel."
Soul's weakest smoke, broken spirit's harbor,
a life sans light, a drug-induced torpor.

Then Ariadne,
played by Theseus, stumbled upon me
passed out more than asleep.
Out of the Athenian's devious plan
asleep, safe, unaware, father damned.

She laid bare beside me, eternally.
Aware, longer—sober days.
Ariadne stays.

"Close to being consumed,
apathy was my altar.
Self-pity, a pathetic, fetid womb."
Bacchus stretches his back.
The man blows smoke:
"One thing coaxed me out of that tomb,"
His eyes hovered over his ocean view.
"Peaceful, humble, healthy, subdued,
respite enjoyed by few.
Ariadne, I stand a half man
for you."

Good folks:
I did not expire
in the addled by-and-by
because death-by-cliché
is the worst way to die.

Wolf

Be it Beowulf
or Virginia Woolf,
heroism
in my undrowned life
lifting rocks
from deep
pockets.

Not heroic,
deaf against silence,
wonderfully made, unafraid,
content
and undulant.

I *might* be that bird
dancing while
casting a net for people.
No cry. No foul.
No church.
Wrong derby.
I am a monstrous barn owl.

Wear the hat and cravat
of a bona fide man.
The smell of leather,
the sternum
pregnant
with laughter.

Be it Beowulf
or Virginia Woolf—
be Beethoven,

sitting up,
deciding solitude
is company
enough.

Hideaway Highway Love Songs
Half notes scored whole.

Let's ride divine. Defiant, not reliant
on the mystic Dixie.
Joan Baez
gently drives us down
to Nashville, Asheville,
and New Orleans.
An expanse of hums.

Towns made of sound,
shady family and pierced strangers
at low tide.
You, my special Joni Mitchell,
the South is our
river to skate away on.

Miles behind us
and miles within us,
the past wears out.
A highway *Wuthering Heights*,
no life by lies or lust or gun.
Not hunted or hounded
by a harsh sun.

You slip into French,
hyacinth in your hair.
Our honkytonk lexicon
speaks of us expelled,
compelled to coo
in tall grass, by the creek,
obscured beneath
the tops of broad trees.

We shimmy from our
delta-wide duvet
to dance, kiss, and caress.
We match: My bare feet,
your summer dress.

Hummingbirds and Robber Barons

Hummingbirds glint
like blades.
My best guess
is that God designed them
to cut the hold of mathematics
from the fowl's small wings.

...

Possums squirrel through trash.
Last night they
smashed, squalled, and hissed.
A bear arrived and bandits,
a quiet riot
of robber barons, dined.

In the early hours,
bearded vandals,
zip up,
regroup
and vanish.

The Sky is a Nightgown

Bring the sky down
in a nightgown.
Foggy ripples
of fall's first cold
choke off the harbor.
Shafts of pine trees—
slick life
still wet.

The mist is a gauzy cloth
that rubs green out of everything.
An old summer
lost its virginity.
Those hours
are seeded cloths,
crinkled
underfoot:
The frozen night.

...

Dark, forceful
2:00 AM fits
tightly between mountains,
into a small town.
A wolf pushes through
pine needles.
Fur trimmed back
by want,
the first thaw—
the first shot at it.

Forefinger into red clay,
rich earth, fertile,
curiously unfrozen:
Sugar, Jack Frost
ain't got shit on you.

Gaudi

for Jon Tribble

Eating lettuce and bland nuts,
he used nature to sculpt
outrageous shapes.
Crosses and windows bejeweled,
gaudy on the Spanish skyline.

Hungry, devout architect,
eyes on a bizarre deity,
his last attempt at a temple
is a castle of comedic figures.
It stands an insect's chapel,
or a dying beehive.

Spires and serpent scales
twist the mind to turn one way,
then fail to follow
his construction
that comes off less
a Christian affair,
more a place of pagan prayer.

Revisited & Restless

Eerie affairs between shadows
devoid of moon jewels.
Lumbering naked with laundry, God unbinds
my wings to fly inside,
reinvented less tawdry.

An avuncular space maws open and swallows
the Mountain King.
With Grieg I regularly walk. In rest we sing
and talk.

Winking, slinking,
hot rails, sleepless spells
revenge when revenge singes
a conflicted man's lineage.
A favor never forgotten.

Now—*silence*—not a myth.
Scatter ills and instill a spine.
A defiant cry. *Choose.* Chalk lines cannot
define what will not
lay down.

A place to pause. Loop one arm,
and then the other, through straps
dusted by comets.
Morning handcrafts a ladder to climb away on.

Big Dad's Death Won't Let Me Rest

In Roland Tire
I brood in the waiting room.
An old television
talks aliens and pyramids.
I spar with my scary
ability to stay angry.
Cardinals
beat wings
against the window.

A Lucky Strikes calendar
cradles impossibly happy girls.
They promise, "The smoother taste
is a lady's favorite."
Read to shreds,
copies of *Time, People,*
and *Guidepost Magazine.*

Not my grandfather's dealership.
This joint's run by a ginger,
in Jasper
jiving with tire rotations
and an oil change.

But the power tools, the sound,
remind me of Big Dad.

…

Air-powered, *whining* power tools:
Whizzing, whine-whine-whine!
Reminiscent of summer chores,

years ago, struggling
up a ladder.
Struggling.

At night,
stripped naked
beneath the club house awning.
Skinny-dipping alone
in a dark pool.
Camel Wides
in the dark
of a townhouse.
Foolish years.
…

At forty-five my quiet defiance
expires.
Big Dad's dead.
Unheard by the deceased.

        The lion, the tiger, and me -
        pile us all atop
        something noble.
        A song that sticks
        in the quiet.

I am the bum
bearing down,
a jagged man
running
from the ghost-clown.
I wish you
the worry
that wears me out.

Granny and Me: Lindale, Georgia 1998–99

Living in Lindale—one year,
a few miles
from Booger Holler—
small rooms, two souls,
no air conditioner,
wood furnace,
initials etched in a chair.

A single sister
from a house of brothers,
Granny grew into
a rowdy, laughing,
shoulder-punching
wild-haired Hazie.
She spoiled me.
Spoiled us all.

She hacked off the head
of every
copperhead.
She was safe.
We talked through
two hundred sunsets,
and one, bad night.
Granny said,
"Let go and let God,"
but we both held on.

She told me,
"Love is better spent
than saved."

Doting, fussing lunchroom lady,
we watched
Wheel of Fortune, Jeopardy,
and *Unsolved Mysteries.*

An Ode to Autism

Almost awake, floating between snow leopards, I slumber under Great-Grandfather's desk. A reptilian child, my mind fixed, unreasonable, incinerating, dreaming, unaware of the *Great Out There*: no squelching school buses, no crowds, no close talkers.

Sleep: *Foggy banks of sleep*. A great tank below, enormous koi (blue and yellow) circle slow-moving light. I, the man, am undetectable neon.

An invisible man, unstuck, in-luck, steering his steam-powered riverboat straight into
white noise—*comfortable*.

…

Awake, uninhibited and un-drunk.

My mind? *Where is my mind?* Typically, war-torn mountains—more in adored valleys these days.

In a diner: People off buses, babies cry, and the sound of chewing.

Aware of what everyone's doing.

On the kitchen's window ledge sits sugar, salt, and cinnamon—content in place. The waitress bats her lashes. I imagine sparrows in her eyes—*flirting* someone tells me. Missed but un-mourned.

Every nook and corner, song, ring tone, and odor—this moment in vivid technicolor. Awake. (*Breathe.*) Serene against a riot. Don't grow blue.

God whispers, "I am in autism, too."

My Father & I Share Seasons

A ruby ribbon
of fleeting light
over pecan trees.
Branches vacant,
shell-wrapped gifts.
Dad and I see the sky.

Work
with necessary silences.
We ticked-off our time
felling trees,
learning landlines,
keeping bees.

Pop pointed out:
Good luck is a lie.
Success is a soap opera.
Wisdom is freedom earned.
If it wants your worry,
piss on it.

Rough Trim

The armrest
combats coitus.
Just as my guard does,
fries fall.

The cracks between seats
leave vents
for old pens,
roach clips,
and gold tokens
of unbroken sobriety.

Too little allowed
in a truck
not loud enough
for rough trim.
Smoker's lungs
whine like a tired dog.

In the trunk
there's an urge
to test the flavor
of five-year-old gum.
She swallowed
what I left unbitten.

Bach, a Few Notes

Bach, an infinite serenade
to the moon.
Do not play
to please the world.

The nocturne a narrative:
Creation,
no bad temper,
no sour youth,
no unfulfilled old age.

Man aware of God,
wailing babies,
frightened mothers,
curl
through church pews.
Limbs lacking spiteful bones
take the grave
with grace.

Organ pipes
propel
beyond confines
of a boy.
The new stranger
we need.

On You

I shine the sun
and polish the moon
to focus all light
on you.

Wanting Romulus

Wanting Romulus
grows into an olive tree.
Fruit refuses to ripen.
The ruler's homespun
clothes are cut from the wolf
who nursed him.
Hewn to each other always,
the two chew bitter roots.

In the 1980s, Remus
shared stitches with Romulus.
Young mouths unburdened
by fear of looking foolish,
not certain
how the dead frown
when we speak.

Romulus confesses
his quest for fame
became stained hands
that slapped his brother's
pale face.
Murder made the news.
Pillars stabbed
into red earth.

A king's kids:
The result of arduous work
and its consequence.
Homeless,
old hats left
on a hook
to regain the sky.

Sunset Calling Over Seven Thousand Miles

Virago—dominate the expanse, reaching, wrenching
the horizon loose.
Torn from its moorings, cascading
tap dancing, toned, emboldened
except what she carves
out for others.
Gnarled through fisted hands
the past, the first days,
forcing elasticity into time.

Concrete shoes: *C'mon girl, they don't fit.*
Lakes, the deepest hands go
into earth, to water, to be seen, noticed,
lightened, untethered from any
harmful star.
Three hours is too long.
Distance doesn't grant
a pass on closeness.

...

Diamonds knitted
into scarves
she wears from years
where easy problems
sank wildly titanic plans.
Brown shoes with a black suit,
old social events where neither of us
darned a damn.
Gloves, anorexia, drug addiction, constant
motion, holding rails
attached to nothing.

Highway to airplane, phrases, exact recollection,
free-falling—no blasted pieces
oozing, unforgiving. No knots
to fight in this release of blood
and semen.

Untalented in cost effective options, not the ant—
but neither the frittering cricket.
Parables, morals, morays—you stay there,
hands in your pockets.
Pull out candy and prayers.

Natural breaks, delicate tenants:
I've no complaints. Challenged to speak better of you,
no—the challenge sits in my need for you.
Backed up on heels, broke.
Chest worked, you—Olympic, gymnastics, dance,
gyms, sponsors (not the Alcoholics Anonymous flavor—bad coffee
and cigarettes). You took to television,
bones chipped, *The Reinventive Years.*

…

Different words: On hands and knees,
displeased by affairs not tucked in neatly.
Construct the yard, the trees, 90-degree angles,
grass cut and tucked behind lamb's ear.
Awfully sincere in sunny situations after a storms
wore us from jealousy.

Thorns exist for no reason
but that isn't proof life is cruel.
You: Circle 8s of conversation, phones,

computers, *Zoom* (I swear they're responsible.)
Smiles captured, *seizing* the outer points
across soft pewter.
Calendars nearly pointless.

No concerts.
No trips.
No easy afternoons.

...

Acting, enacted by the congress of balance,
a virago—alone.

Virago on the Ocean

A *virago* enjoys smooth indigo,
cool her knack
for knee-jerking push-back.
Seasoned and therein lies
why the captain adores her.
Four unquestionable words
cement the lady as his crew:
I believe in you.

There's good business
in smart romance.
Smooth slinking woman forward,
a waltz, not a flighty, foolish dance.
Without an argumentative tide,
Costa Rica ripples off
the starboard side.
Two twist in an onboard tempest,
now listing
toward mankind.

They get close enough
to smell the sand,
but instead, muscle on
a deserted land.
The two fondu in a valley,
an Eden beside a NASCAR rally
that splays open an orchard of orange, fig,
and apple trees.

It's too soon for tourists, shrieking children,
and mushroom-tripping.
Tomorrow will be about sneaking out,
and skinny dipping.

I Remember the Earth

For behold, I create new heavens and a new earth; And the former things will not be remembered or come to mind.
Isaiah 65:17

I remember the Earth.
I imagine her a harsh matron. She snaps string green beans between the idols of Hermes and Hercules. It is impossible to think of the Earth without her face. A spell cast beyond our embryonic farewell. The Earth, like the womb with a view, the one-room apartment it took eleven hours to leave, and I carved "Brooks was here," down her spine and uterine wall when it was clear my exile.

The Earth hasn't, God hasn't, life-begetting-life hasn't forged a keenness for humans. What's the stuff that spins us into a thicket? *Eros.* I met her in an emotionally crippled condition, under the influence, under bridges, preoccupied by attrition. Great faith creates Hume's causality (perhaps "purgatory" because mankind tends to fuck up perfection), is in this building, a few rooms away, probably petrified to share her insight or career while I sit here serene and sincere.

Hawaiian Nightmarchers, broken horses, rocket launchers, Okinawa, an extraction plan in Atlanta (a second freedom ride from me)—my harlequin idea of heroism bent on a cauli-flowered ear. The cosmos clapped out lightning rods, Cape Cod, and Alderaan. We stand straight with our backs to old promises, forgotten rain, and over time your scarves and forever-snoozed morning alarms tie off my addictions, the contradictions I root up like rubies. Deception was the strongest, tallest wall.

Not at all, it is a prison silent and savage. Our language smeared like lipstick on a mirror saying, "Go! Run *now!*" The "I" of the covetous

me, the boy in the mid-70s set free, grown into a third person perspective with room for two, baggage abandoned on the curb. (Do not pry or disturb.)
I remember the Earth.

One Word

Sacrifice

Cowboy Blue Crawford's Salvation:
His Shadow Contains a Man

A man stands in the indention
left by murder of goodwill.
Stagnant, perished for lack purpose.
Incivility, droll, dopamine-induced
dilation of the eyes, haunted,
hinged to a hurricane:
Cowboy Blue Crawford.

Nature,
there is nothing mortal
that can spoil the uprising
of Mokosh.

Not an allegory,
but an explosion throughout the South
that incinerates the common place
as well as man's unquestioning
tendency to hate it.
Wendigo and thistled dope
thin his Miss Dixie.

Whimsy, behind the Piggly Wiggly,
abreast of knotted snakes.
This atom bomb embodies no soul or sinew.
Unrest is not yours to execute.

...

Morning astride Miss Dixie.
She, the tool useless
to fix sin Blue won't refuse.

Boxes of bullets, forever-infused blood,
blueberries in cream
enjoyed on a quiet road.

Hands, nails too long
for witchcraft.
Lips too dark to speak of it.
Baton Rouge refuses to release Miss Dixie.
Cupped like baby birds, her memory
is to Blue like nesting.

...

In North Georgia
he gave up his wife's ghost,
a host of beleaguered friends,
and flights of spirits.
After her he, and his team
sprint, tag-out/tag-in:
savage instincts
regardless of good drugs
or open charges.

...

Blue leaves New Orleans
crazy laced-up watching Lily sashay
in leather pants.
Father Hammer entranced
in Kenkage's casual
style of sharp objects.
Without fear the flock would think
their faith in escape untrue.
Centered by Blue

iniquity, weak and infinite.

Blue, swamp heart,
his two rooms are right
as reimbursement.
A chair, a bed,
and nightstand.
Love is an elusive lie of want.

To a Childhood Infatuation

Insane lady, lazy Penelope,
you—the best,
bad omen.
Your atonement
not on account
or about
me.

I can't buy you
no BMW,
no home in Paris,
but I can afford
the energy
to move
away from you.

This poem is an epitaph
to a childhood infatuation
you refuse to lose.

Bad Poems

Bad poems
are unlucky pennies.
They keep turning up.

To sell this poem
is trading a dead puppy
for an abortion.
Practicing the performance
of bad poetry
bitches
to the back
of a deaf man's head.

Not to write
is worse.
Good or bad,
the practice
prevents
sepsis of the senses.
The gods abhor
neglect.
Abhor repetition.

Bad poems
are unlucky pennies.
They keep turning up.

Roswell's Day of the Dead

Orpheus and Eurydice
think they are free of Hades,
but that is never true.
Canton Street moves:
Families,
classic cars,
us loving in the past.
We danced into *Día de Muertos*.
A dog dies, windchimes.

Before the Corona,
in Havana outside Atlanta,
we walked as the dearly departed.
The small city
opens into aqueducts,
food trucks, breweries,
a cemetery.

Old books, a room,
an ancient man
with dyslexia
and jaundiced eyes.
My kind, my kindred,
he asked me to read Tennyson.

Talk comes easy,
but laughter skipped out.
No family on my side
of the table.
Rented space.

Fourth of Nothing fireworks
frighten us.
The end's not long now.

Nocturne closes,
the town retires.
Crowds, crushed happiness,
far from me.
No interest.
Harangued.

Tomorrow the park reopens,
the symphony played out
to *Día de Muertos.*

How Will I Begin

Sing, sing, sing you precious nightingales. Shoot up, flood the sky
before clouds pour us down.
It is begun.
This is no Friday chaconne, the piece folded three times to pin down
a whole weekend. Dusted, pollen rubbed over denimed knees—the
world easier to breathe
clean through gills in my eyes. Unrushed, eager for sex.

-       *The turn*:

Convince me—tell me about mending sounds. *Create:* Begin,
embrace me, Lawrence Ferlinghetti—to stumble over you, begin
again out of a thorny ditch. Lean into me. The land holds me still.
Begin: Deliver in slivers our safe space, items on a takeout menu.
Poets, not the horrible obligations. Years ahead, sing. Once sung we
are not forgotten.

Skeletons Whisper My Name

I watch Daddy's deal
heal customers' doubt.
A natural, a man
undefeated, unbowed,
cracked where good men fight.

Father and son abide.
Abandoned, our legacy,
staying angry.
Rage, pity—
useless as shoveling rain
with a pitchfork.

Until no rock remains
to pound
into sand,
the land we're left with
needs us.

Do not relent to sorrow.
Drop the Atlas-aching weight.
You do not want it.
I do not want it.

All those cars.
Convertibles without a conscience,
my bones, my marrow.
Veins over a few hundred miles.
Fake hips
and shoulders carry on.

Quiet

Hawks watch
a chicken
without a head
in silence.

...

4 and a half weeks,
a sabbatical.
Romanced in quiet.

In quiet so compelling,
Where have you been?

In the bones
jut spurs
around my forehead.

The science of quiet
insists
I stay away.

Silence from her,

silence from him,

silence from it,

silence from her.

...

Months,
maybe more.
Broken tiles
in the kitchen floor.

Silence.

Lightning Laughter Knitting

Forgive my intrusion.
My mind
minces elsewhere.

War browbeats men
while alive the old man made a way
to see me in a seersucker suit.

Eight weeks
and no one explains the awful getaway.
The focus of my rage stays on the face
of one doctor who dialed up
the ugliest machine,

and smiled while lightning
lit the pity out of me.
The deal was less lightning
for my leaving

the concerning crusade to write
as a career.
I refused, and much of the result
I cannot remember.

Across a Long, Narrow Room

strewn with cords,
a soundboard between us.
Unsteady, me.
Steady, she,
we shake free
of rusty words.

She, unmoved
by the afternoon.
Disparity
between us,
the armor
she wore
up from Florida.

At her core,
a ruby—
a pulsing pear.

Badlands,
a landscape—speaking,
the radio—talk
walking off.

Dust motes
settle as she
nestles
on the floor.

Orchard, Blood & Bone

Permanence, lies
last night.
Your face angst-less
against the pillowcase.

We, two commanding
too close
to occupy the same space.
Fingertips trace
scars—one vertebra,
another.

Lower, where you
tug in, blanket
between us tightly.
Touch lightly.
breathe barely.
Not yet regret.

Impressions:
Sheets meet the morning-
after our bleating
chiseled pretending
into this mess.

Lines from linen
dig in to cut off
contact.
Easy, now cooled.

Remedies exist.
Remembering, I insist.
The bed, the night,
scars.

Airplanes Won't Leave Washington

What if it never happens?
Cigarettes—walk up,
walk back,
obsessively.
Butts thrown
down a drain.

The wings
of all endured
endear themselves
to me.

No fight means
no resolve.
Lay down the blade.
Live, dance, stay.

Requiem for a Raven

Plumage flays me
now from my spine.
Over time.
age fish-scales
around the ribcage.
On the wind I'm swell.
Arms flung out to embrace
the breath
thrust up
from those below.

Raised:
        UP!
    Up;
 up.

Off a ledge
I descend into headwinds.
No debts, scarce stress,
a blackbird.
Tina's *big wheel*
keeps on turning.
Devoid of proud Mary,
still out of tune,
but still—*this*:

A magic trick for nickels,
a stolen
peaceful moment,
thousands of dollars.

I rely on the well of good hope
where I die of thirst.
This is not in my bed.

Cynical in places
bullets go. Upward,
a way home,
over the distracted crowd.

The raven, riven into skin.
A bar
hidden behind
a red phone booth.
I am strong.
Latin binding words.
I belong.

Lift the breeze.
Soft curves we see.
Minutes away.

Girl in my flannel, head down
too thin from war.
I spare no time for you,
nor how deep the scar.

The Songstress

for Angel Snow

Angel Snow: Auburn hair swept back
by a wooden rod
through soft leather.
Un-catchable music,
a lady's metered optimism
planted God in Greece.

Loose bricks, candlesticks,
songs over oceans.
Home from Africa,
night terrors, Alight, intoxicating,
oscillating fans,
good works—
the translucent eye.

For a minute she was Dixie.
"My brother named me Angel."
A second birth.
No second thought.
She is.

Nashville, yoga,
we visit Hindu temples
and a speakeasy.
Indian food below fireflies.
Libations, my harsh creation.
She is free to dine and drink
'til the moon
no longer rounds.

Measuring the Day

In inches
see the shoreline,
the lamplight,
the river.
Moonlight kept
in a tin can,
peppermint sticks.

A long shadow,
cast from
a small corner.
A giant,
taller than
discomfort.

To miles,
miles beyond,
bare chested,
no one
feels cast aside.
This is juvenile.

Long nights
leave footprints.
Sitting in Sandy Springs
repentant,
unclean.
Inches creeping,
lost time.

Jolene

On Interstate 575
she stays
on the tongue
like navel
oranges.

Songs—*Jolene*
on my lips,
and photos of
a heroin addict
tucked in a Gideons Bible.

Lovers
beg juice
from someone
else. We
understandably stray.

Pass from one—
men sense it,
feel it,
aftershave.
Music left for better days.

Chip away at it.
Head back
unowned,
unbowed,
eager not to linger.

Jolene
sounds better
with age.

Common Thoughts

An indelible thumbprint,
a god-marker
on the inside
of your wrist.
Proof of loss
and consequence.

The feeling that
things left unsaid,
or poorly said,
or said at all
fall bare knees
into glass.

A Hairdresser from Ecuador & Barber Named *Holla*

Surgery, shaving away grime.
Slicing away the doomed-by-design,
scents of what idly died.

Carmen: The mane in retrograde.
Charming, soaring, adored from Ecuador—
refined—care and concern.

Holla: Gypsy-tattooed.
The wolf's son, mahogany against the light.
Sandalwood through my beard.

No funerals, no loss, three cultures,
no braiding or shaving in struggle.

Wingless and Dreadful

November hasn't seen her,
but it's only the first.

Scars—a terrible, lasting
word.

Leaves. The verb. Nouns
can't keep rain off paper,
wingless and dreadful.

Beads Threaded through Fingers

The second time
arrives upending
belief in spite
of us.

Unnoticed
on the way
to Emmaus, Ellijay,
Austin.

...

A blue heron glides
across water
forming a sheen
between us
and Ed Gein.

A Child's Drawing Found on the Subway

In innocent hand—a drawing—amok, children play, sisters and a brother, through brambles, snow drifts, dogs, coyotes, drunk mother. Absent father. Stick figures catch fish too frail for food. Crayons feed the artist.

Subway cars blast past, the drawing tears—those children: *I never agreed on kids. Never considered it.* Voices trail off, pieces of lives, the doors close.

Strangers *whoosh* away.

In Jest; the Expanse

The sky, a naked place,
an awful quiet across
four bludgeoned corners.

The jest; the expanse:
I believe in nights.
Rilke, lilac, and lights—
the duende—inspiration and pixie.
Delicious bouquets
Augustus leaves
in the nave.

Incandescent rubles
spark Tesla arcs of diamonds.
Nightlights,
afternoon almost twilight,
the dark
carves out scars
to rub dirt in.

Sit aside Arcade Fire
and dangle a meted sun.
Recollection runs over
hands cupped spilling
marbles rounded with age.

No disease.
No broken tables.
No scathing hours.

Hermes

I lie
shirtless
and sharpened.

Run
along my jawline
a Dominican keeps.

Unsettled,
September blows
butterflies.

Lacking a single fuck,
pronouns
can't establish ownership.

Winged feet
aren't fast enough.

Richmond

Morning, less than early,
more towards noon,
a courtyard—monuments broken, overgrown,
strewn entrails of stone, stricken words—
proud dead—now illegitimate.
Itinerant sons visit,
weep,
and then bury their wounds.

...

No promises. No romance. No phone calls.
This, forgotten, belabored of life—childless.
I bind off, off a young dog, off the backroads
interstate inevitably dies on.

Because I am not there.
The shaved down lack of anything
resembling fairness, equal breakage, the insistence
that my presence
maintains, abrasive.

I told you! (untrue)
Yelled in the street, after me
after Vivaldi's winter
twisted into a symphony
jealousy sparked
off chest and crest off my head.

Not the place
in space that leaves room
for hindsight.

Life without discernable roots
grows ugly truth.

Between two viciously-in-love
a blood orange splits.
Fruit whose pulp carries
your bloated, winey taste

In the Wide Motion of Embraceable Light

No lake to embrace, prisms, glinting spoons filched
at the bottoms
of mussels eaten all summer.
Temper the trap, it's—your—a score
of sweet dispositions.

Hunger, a depth of gnawing
sews news of the blues,
songs belonging to disappointment,
sacrifice, fights with demons,
semen birthing strong women.

Today, a remembering place.
Mortality's ability to numb
or nudge our breed beyond
the finite.

Bones,
metacarpals matted
to California Sober.
Brittle the mind not-so-by-gone
by methamphetamines.
…

The men:
Two—grown and his child—
an unsettled new stance
between bulldogs.

Calamity

If you can't teach me how to fly, teach me how to sing.
—Peter Pan

Van Gogh, God's golden flower,
prolific years, a brother's tears,
sunflower mouths sing
with crooked teeth.
Listening, healed,
flying.

A man insane by angels,
a saint acknowledged by strangers,
we experience stars
          close to earth,
licking the sky,
whether or not
we can
fly.

Our Eyes so Vainly Look

It is difficult to write of words without
describing words.
Poets speak only of poets,
passive aggressive accolades
from a distance.

The same here,
since the previous summer,
faltering,
less-than-dapper; the words,
their clipped, limited power.
Sound slows hours
and stills mountains.

Oyster of Addicted Pearls

In my soul's chewed center is the fox.
Deep-biting elbows, fighting like the third monkey
almost on the ark—just short of saving.

Lungs scorched from oxygen's absence.
The weakness of man plunges me deeper,
a foolish flesh refusing its fur.

Less than a monkey, much more a money-bound thing –
a lazy Essene out of water,
drowning—the fox.

My disease in an oyster
of addicted pearls. I sink,
ocean above unbroken.

Naiveté, Girl in Play

The girl-child
picks snapdragons.
Lavender, less tragic
opens in her.

In the spring?
A white, cotton dress,
peals of laughter,
skimming across water,
joy, carelessness, naiveté,
the girl.

The Middle East:
Unmolested, laden in honey,
unfabricated, descriptions
of youth and war—
similar, dour notes.

Guiltless, godless, motion fiddles
with time and its passing.
Mitochondrial comets,
fecund wit, homes
without locked doors.

Natasha's Indelible Pedestal

for Natasha Shneider & Alain Johannes

"An M For Orpheus"
by Alain Johannes

1.

My insolence cloaked
In innocence
Somehow, is erring
Down in this underworld
(Not the one of
Myths passed down
From eons of
Patterns perceived)
But the other where...
Reflections dance
In the mind's eye
Becoming sentience
Transfixed on a game
Of shadows
Inside a labyrinth
The object
To birth synaptic branches
Voraciously reaching
Towards
Purest chaos

2.

And you again
Opposing beauty
A sightless slight
Comfortable and terrifying
Miming a death march
Of countless steps
Leading to dimmest light
Never brightening
Imprisoned in a tunnel
That doesn't exist

3.

I will save your breath
From eternal exhale
Even if,
By breaking first law
Untying all knots
Reversing fated flaw,
I suffer the consequence...
To be no more when
You finally wake

...

No longer pulled, plied, confounded, falsely worshipped, indulged, fooled into blindness: unwound, unwatched, unkempt by time— aloft, alight—no seafood, medicines from family-old faith, a mother, mermaid, and the mountains.

Words bend in my head, clunky, misused, misunderstood, poorly maintained, shoes that pinch my toes - hands carving into hard ground to exact a language.

You: The scaffolding, screaming stars, pinpricks shot around the moon, once a part of us, now pitted, defaced, littered by ghosts. You. Outside the wheelhouse klickety-klack, grunting, suspicious— unclaimed, separated, emerged.

Museums, tearful babies, dinosaurs, trinkets—3 cops in SUVs digging in the back of a Civic. Swings. Capped, pink toes in flip flops and forehead furrowed over texts from an ex-something. Nothing completely easy, paradise vipers, apples, and pomegranates. Hades has seasons.

Our spring sours in summer, reaches barren branches to sew fruit heavy in flesh. Bent over Christmas, 13 years ago known on riverbanks, large stones thrown at a man-child, the decision our volition is worth burning the office—unavoidable.

Alain exists for Eurydice.

Found, the Dark Wood

Unbound stands trees, boundaries diverge, light through keyholes
unlock the Baroque wardrobe full of wolves—muted dreams remind
us, Roswell Road is an eon away from Ellijay.

Rooms held by curtains, kindling—lines tying down plans that
crumble under scrutiny. Lifted—pilfered 'cause "stolen" sounds bad.
Lifted, un-left, new clothes, tighter skin, tattoos, new stories with
weathered friends.

Experimental, purses on hooks the stall doors hold low enough
thieves risk fingers to reach. Yelling—unattractive introspection,
indecent detection (habits), xenophobia, crossed media—Nova Scotia
—battles built up to unmoor the shipwrecks we depend on.

Bars bend under pressure. The clientele crutch themselves against *the
other, the not us, the always welcome with silence*—don't rewrite or
retire what we hope won't leave obsolete.

Try to leave out the hills, city, hurt kids, hurting skids that birth the
best TV. Legends leave chasms where our forgiveness skittered into
shadows people won't point out. Cantos strewn across feathered
pillows, temporary scars, bedspreads, ceiling fans, tile floors, and a
lawnmower cutting in circles.

An Arch Over the Earth

We tread water.
Waves forget.
Rounding horizons
upend purple dawns
to shed light on
teacups.

Blithe friends lag.
Amicable daemons dangle
    down the string
                of a kite.
Arching across longitude
to connect you.

Come into the Earth
from wanting.
Nature—the knack
to lose heart in sand.
12 steps better
than September.
Hard rain grows
and we cherish roses.

I Miss My Dog

We struggled into love. A sunlit promise that shook out by winter. My dog Daisy, the only cog in that frigid machine wound in my favor. Storms stayed. Stars burnt out. The day chewed by spite. The moon too scared to shine. We incinerated and I survive as a country song: *She kicked me out during Corona and her cold heart kept my dawg.*

I miss her—*Daisy*. Amazing, that one. A brindle, I spindled up in her; a hound I found astounding. Smart. *Me*, not so much. I had a hunch. A mother, son, and live-in teen—three. Daisy sat beside me while they whispered. There was one, two, three, and now a fourth wealth, old man.

Your son ruled the court and my candor about it destroyed our manor. *Daisy*, stolen. Dysfunction: You asked, "How much is your inheritance?" "How much is your *mom* worth?" The cutting, hungry, reptilian brain thought it sane your son facilitated an affair. "It wasn't an affair. We weren't married."

You burned my gifts, glared—without a word—stared: Letters from jail, photos, my books—fingerprints you fancied me.

The hammock hugged us while you hated me. No more sandwiches taken to a miserable job. Now, in suspension, your Laurentian landscape is a wasteland no longer across my shoulders. There were no victims. Trust, more purloined coins in the gut of a greedy, digging beast. Brutalized. Misinformed. Incestuous.

A forceful need makes you mean, your dream, a practiced knack for cleaning sheets so my long shadow makes room for his small frame. *Money*—your home's throne. Not my home. This is not my team. "It's not an affair. We weren't married," your voice guilty, but no

79

admission of guilt because the silt in your soul's seat grinds in from abandonment. An infection you insist is your best lesson.

Not my circus. *Not* my monkeys...

...but I *really* miss my dog.

Break from Mythology

Still smoking cigarettes,
the smallest syllable—
a larger size
than
I.

Spliced

I am the eye
of a bad actor.
An iris-adapted
instinct
on edge.

Pen the hour,
the pulse,
what is holy,
what we see.

Malleable men
and women,
their usefulness,
by rain crested
off the next hill.

Janus

The monster, the betrayer,
when to be monstrous.

Hail dents
puddles.
Knuckles rib
into skin.
Doorknobs
never draw blood.

The laurels of a good life
go to the victor
of awful things.
Work saves men
bent in vicious circles.

Blood,
a smearing
of lipstick.
A knife fight, a lonely night,
words on words
on words.

Couched in Gossamer Flesh

Flights, nuanced evenings couched in gossamer flesh. Anorexic, tragic, an unfolded map—a woman wears a dead stare. Stairs sans a crystal chandelier or tribute band, surrendered tickets, identification, yoga pants, Alma Coffee—sweaters just enough for spring shouldering divorce, children, debt, contentment in the eldest away on scholarship.

Bilingual but unable to talk about sex in either. A glass of water, sugar, irritation, impatience, oblivious to weather and bad lyrics.

An Audi A7 in her crypt gaze. Through me, Old Dirty Bastard, the whole Wu-Tang—a tiger, Afro Samurai, anime in Sturgill Simpson—dice of my life spat across a parking lot.

A5 outside Ingles, Porsche whose ancient owner said, "You ain't old enough to own this stuff." *Facts.*

Eyes, always eyes—windows, mirrors, portals - the darker the more they've seen. DMX on her stereo there's a passport and plans for Cairo—she refuses to explain.

Clouds of ones and zeroes blow over identical mountains, bison, trailer parks, and Social Circle. Presidents, volleyball, Moleskines, charcoal pencils, bills paid in ink beneath bifocals on a broken nose. This ankle, artwork in Vinings, The Kills: Fingertips tap a spot on a map (Nashville)—*Something's got a hold on me.*

The kitchen: Espresso in two cups. A stunning lady, lissome at 31-years—an empress in no dress. Living room, *Candyman*, dancing, demons slipping between us to sit in the kitchen. Gravity, motion of too many years and two roads dirty with an unattainable dawn. Six weeks spent slinking into something new.

From the Kitchen Table

Fresh flowers, dying ones, decay in space between us. This chair and four walls last as wallpaper fades. Time dotted by ex-boyfriends knocking, tick-tocking we smoked pot and forgot. Our epic error etched into glass overlooking country too poor to pay attention. Talk of kitchens makes a metaphor for what fails to gel.

YouTube videos on lawnmower repair, a day in Atlanta, back to address the gym before I fucking kill somebody. A wreck of us, the fever, veins, an old mirror in front of our naked carnage—broken bed and haunted staircase. A buffoon and the defeated politician vote both ways. Sin the same way. Secrets shake screws loose as the booze hidden in the kitchen.

Entropy of one man in the middle of a million bullshit things to distract from the fact he can't find center. Core locked in constant snarl. Resolved not to window-look, but inward. Hoping to tumble, obesity grounds your daughter. In the bedroom, sex sweats forgetfulness into the fact you have a stack of toothbrushes, stash of men's clothes, bongs thrown in your yard.

Nights of outside-sitting, safe from COVID, tired of it and still wearing a mask because it's good business. A virus politicked into ignorant resolve. Banksy, sex, laundry, daydreaming. Your swagger stopped traffic. We beat downtown to death. Two trips to Lexington. It was cool to sit with you.

What we do is important. Widowed lines jut off paper, dangling, blocked. *Widowed*— lines, people, causes, pets—an assumption none of it fits. I cinch the suture where a new wound seeps. Our kitchen: The first place people feel, see, or think about.

Aries

Centered left of you,
not in you—the malformed child;
an anchor in the hallway.
Fields, the cotton and corn,
across Europe—
slippage, carnage, aircraft carriers—
west of the Mississippi, uncomplicated
long fingers.

(Sex.)

Taut neck muscles, desert goes out,
bedsheets of parents
with a king size bed.
Children push their arms up, eyes shut to
brutal noon.
Midday rains hammers.

Playgrounds, greyhounds,
dogs leap for their owners.
Three boys work together.
Commotion, interruptions,
assumptions of what one does
seven thousand miles away.

Acorns, Halloween,
and unfinished stories
stuff envelopes
in hopes messages
make it into the proper box.

You slow the small hands
of a perfectly wound clock.

The Barn Behind Me

Two large windows from a loft-leveled point of view:
mountains through birch.
A small table, couch, bed, me—quasi-contemporary Gregorian chant
below where a woman reclines,
my raven redeemed.
Hail pecks against glass.
One bird, no dog, and a routine.

…

The Big Lebowski went on about a carpet. Philip Seymour Hoffman
died of heroin. Best friends came and went between routine
screenings.
Heroin stole lovers. The movie gives up their ghosts.
Haunted with an eye on Emeya.

…

Winter: dissenter among hot girl summers. Generation X,
Millennials,
I think there's a "z" in there somewhere…
…the separation sits between us and Boomers.
Bad jokes. Resentments choke.
Worse kids. Broken trends.
I don't feel old. Near 50—a man, bold,
arresting what Rilke burst in fountains.

…

Walking, whether in the mind, across time, or in line at Quick
Trip—

—   I am walking, aura-gripped by Catherine.
When one only thinks things one only has thoughts.
The lip of a water pump sticks in cold.
The handle smells of sandalwood.
Long weekend lovers
share water in winter hard to draw out.

The Author

CLIFFORD BROOKS is a poet, teacher, and founder of the Southern
Collective Experience. He has two previous collections of poetry and
a chapbook. Find out more at www.cliffbrooks.com and
www.southerncollectiveexperience.com.